Investigating Weather

C.B. Green and R.M. James

Nelson

Thomas Nelson and Sons Ltd
Nelson House   Mayfield Road
Walton-on-Thames   Surrey
KT12 5PL   UK

51 York Place
Edinburgh
EH1 3JD   UK

Thomas Nelson (Hong Kong) Ltd
Toppan Building 10/F
22A Westlands Road
Quarry Bay   Hong Kong

Thomas Nelson Australia
102 Dodds Street
South Melbourne
Victoria 3205
Australia

Nelson Canada
1120 Birchmount Road
Scarborough   Ontario
M1K 5G4   Canada

ACKNOWLEDGEMENTS

The weather forecasts on p. 25 are reproduced by permission of the
following: Express Newspapers; Mirror Group Newspapers; News
Group Newspapers; Times Newspapers, based on information
supplied by the Meteorological Office.

Illustrations by CMA, Plymouth, Denby Designs and Terry Bambrook

Cover photography: Studio 4, Exeter

Contents

What Is Weather?   4

Elements of the Weather   6

Temperature   8

Investigating Temperature   10

Rainfall   12

Investigating Rainfall   14

Clouds   16

Investigating Clouds   18

Wind   20

Investigating Wind   22

Weather Forecasting   24

Investigating Weather Forecasting   26

Useful Data Collection and Classification Sheets   28

Notes for Teachers   30

What is Weather?

Day-to-day changes in the air at any particular place are called 'weather'. Weather is made up of temperature, rainfall, wind and clouds. The study of weather is called meteorology. The scientists who study weather and try to forecast its changes are called meteorologists.

The weather changes daily and from season to season so it can have many effects upon us. It is part of our lives and we have to adapt to it in many different ways.

Activities

A   Dressing for the weather

1   The clothes people wear are often influenced by the weather. Look at the pictures showing people dressed for different types of weather. Which person has more layers of clothes?
2   Describe the type of weather each is dressed for and explain why they are dressed in this way.
3   Why do we not wear gloves and scarves in the summer?

Wool hat
Scarf
Dufflecoat
Wool gloves
Wellington boots

Dressed for snow in Britain

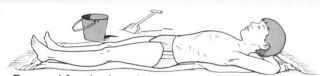

Dressed for the beach in sunny weather

B   Building for the weather

1   Buildings are designed for different types of weather. How is your own home designed to keep you warm and dry during cold, wet weather, yet cool when it is hot?
2   Look at the three houses below. What kind of weather would you expect to find in the places where such houses are built? How is each house designed for particular weather conditions?
3   In some countries where there is cold weather and snow the houses have very steep roofs. In other places houses have strong gently sloping roofs which allow the snow to stay on them. Can you think of the reasons?
4   Why would it be unsuitable for houses in Britain to have roofs like house (b)?

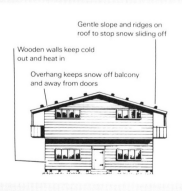
Gentle slope and ridges on roof to stop snow sliding off
Wooden walls keep cold out and heat in
Overhang keeps snow off balcony and away from doors

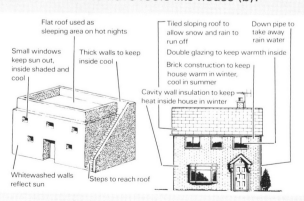
Flat roof used as sleeping area on hot nights
Small windows keep sun out, inside shaded and cool
Thick walls to keep inside cool
Whitewashed walls reflect sun
Steps to reach roof
Tiled sloping roof to allow snow and rain to run off
Down pipe to take away rain water
Double glazing to keep warmth inside
Brick construction to keep house warm in winter, cool in summer
Cavity wall insulation to keep heat inside house in winter

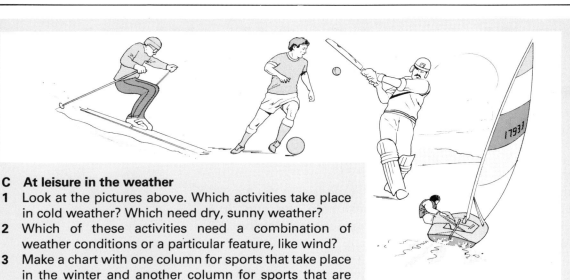

C At leisure in the weather

1 Look at the pictures above. Which activities take place in cold weather? Which need dry, sunny weather?

2 Which of these activities need a combination of weather conditions or a particular feature, like wind?

3 Make a chart with one column for sports that take place in the winter and another column for sports that are played in the summer. Write down as many as you can think of.

D Eating habits and the weather

1 What do you usually eat and drink when the weather is cold and wet?

2 When are you likely to eat ice cream and drink cool drinks?

3 Plan a meal for a cold winter day and another for a warm summer day.

E Summary

1 Name the four elements which make up our weather.

2 What do we mean by the word meteorology?

3 What is a meteorologist?

4 Our weather is different in each of the four seasons. What are their names?

5 Copy and complete the chart below to show how the weather affects your life in each season.

Season	Typical weather	Clothes	Games	Food	Home
Winter	cold snow frost	overcoat gloves	football hockey	stews soup	heating on windows closed

6 Would the conditions you wrote in the chart be the same for each day of the season?

7 Write your own paragraph to show how the weather affects people at work. Here are some clues. Think of the work a farmer has to do on the farm. A North Sea fisherman will be affected by snow and ice. Frost in spring is a problem to a fruit farmer. What problems does fog cause to people who use roads and airports? How does a strong wind cause difficulties for lorry-drivers?

Elements of the Weather

As we have seen, the weather is made up of a number of elements.

Temperature

This is the warmth or coldness that we feel in the air. The warmth that is in the air comes from the sun. It is measured with a thermometer in degrees Celsius (°C), usually called degrees centigrade.

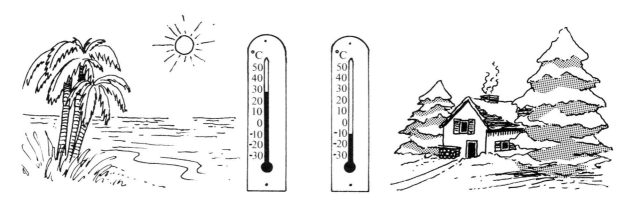

Clouds, mist, fog, dew

The air always contains moisture which is known as water vapour. When air cools, tiny drops of water form. (You can see this for yourself by putting a glass of iced water in a warm room. Very small droplets of water will form on the outside of the cold glass.) These drops of water form clouds. Water vapour that forms clouds close to the ground is called mist or fog. At night water vapour condenses on the cool ground to form dew.

Rainfall, snow, hail, sleet

All forms of moisture that fall to the ground are called precipitation. If there is a lot of moisture in the air the drops of water may become too heavy for the clouds and fall as rain. If it is very cold the moisture may freeze into ice crystals and fall as snow or sleet. Precipitation is measured in millimetres (mm).

Wind

Wind is the movement of air from one place to another. Wind speed is usually measured in kilometres per hour (km/h).

The weather map

Information about the weather is recorded on a weather map. This information is collected from many different sources and includes details of rainfall, temperature, direction and force of wind and the amount of sunshine. We often use a weather forecast to help us plan the following day's activities.

Symbols on a weather map

Symbols are used on weather maps to illustrate the type of weather we can expect. Some of them are illustrated below.

Weather symbols

⑨	Temperature (9°C)
㉒→	Wind speed and direction (20 km/hr)
☁	Cloud
⛅	Cloudy with some sunshine
☀	Sunny, clear skies
🌧	Heavy rain
⛈	Thunder and lightning
🌨	Snow

Weather forecast: Map A

Weather forecast: Map B

Today's Forecast

It will be a cooler day. By morning _____ will reach Wales and the M_____, some of it heavy; it will work its way northwards to southern and central S_____, but the far _____ should remain _____. The _____ coast will remain dull and misty with some _____ patches, with temperatures reaching only ___°c. Brighter weather will spread eastwards, but there could be heavy showers with even hail and _____ in W_____.

Activities

1. Look carefully at the weather forecast in map A. Copy and complete the forecast using these words: dry, rain, Wales, north, thunder, 11°C, Scotland, east, Midlands, fog.
2. What is the highest recorded temperature on map A?
3. What is the lowest recorded temperature on map A?
4. What is the wind speed off the west coast of Scotland on map A?
5. What do you think the following day's weather will be like in the Midlands and Northern England? There is a clue in the last sentence of the forecast.
6. Look at maps A and B. Which of the two days was the warmer?
7. Where on map B would you visit for: (a) sunbathing?   (b) sailing?
8. Which coast was coolest on both days? Can you explain why?
9. These two forecasts are for two days in the same week. What does this tell us about Britain's weather?
10. Look carefully at the forecast for map A then try to write your own forecast for map B.

Temperature

Temperature is a measure of warmth and coldness. Where we live and how we feel will influence our idea of what is warm and what is cold, so in order to have an accurate measurement of temperature we use a thermometer which shows degrees Celsius (or centigrade). (You should not use a thermometer with a Fahrenheit scale, °F.)

How we feel and where we live affect our idea of temperature

Here is an experiment to show that we cannot use our senses to measure temperature.

Take three bowls of water, one cold, one as hot as you can bear, and one warm. Arrange as shown in the diagram below. Put one hand in the cold water and the other in the very hot water. After half a minute transfer both hands into the warm water. Both hands are now in water of the same temperature. What do you notice? Does this help to explain why we need to use a thermometer to measure temperature?

How does each hand feel?

Warning   Do not use water so hot that it scalds you.

How do they feel now?

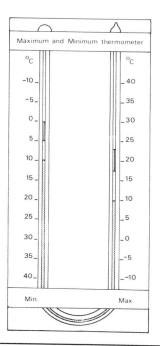

A thermometer is used when an accurate measurement of temperature is needed. In weather forecasts the temperatures given always refer to how warm it will be in the shade.

A maximum and minimum thermometer

This records the highest (maximum) and lowest (minimum) temperature in any one day. It contains mercury and alcohol. (Alcohol is used to record low temperatures because it does not feeze.) The mercury and alcohol move as the temperature changes and push two metal springs, called indexes, along the tubes. The indexes stay at the highest points they reach even after the liquids have moved back. The highest and lowest temperatures can be seen when the recording is taken; this should be done at the same time each day. Readings are taken at the bottom edge of the indexes. When the temperature has been recorded a magnet is used to reset the indexes.

Day	Max.°C	Min.°C	Day	Max.°C	Min.°C	Day	Max.°C	Min.°C
1	20	10	11	16	10	21	20	9
2	16	10	12	18	12	22	20	8
3	16	9	13	16	6	23	15	12
4	19	12	14	16	10	24	13	11
5	18	12	15	15	6	25	20	9
6	17	6	16	16	5	26	21	11
7	22	9	17	18	8	27	14	9
8	23	16	18	17	8	28	19	6
9	19	12	19	20	5	29	20	13
10	18	9	20	20	10	30	16	11

Maximum and minimum temperatures recorded in June

A class of pupils made these temperature recordings during the month of June by recording the maximum and minimum temperatures each day.

Activities

A By looking carefully at the figures for June you should be able to discover the answers to these questions.

1 What was the highest maximum temperature recorded in June? On which day was this?

2 What was the lowest maximum temperature recorded in June?

3 What was the lowest minimum temperature in June? On which day was this recorded?

4 How many days had temperatures above 18°C?

5 How many nights had temperatures below 10°C?

6 Was June a warm or cold month? How can you tell? Write one sentence to describe the weather during June.

7 How might a Bedouin and an Eskimo comment on these temperatures in June?

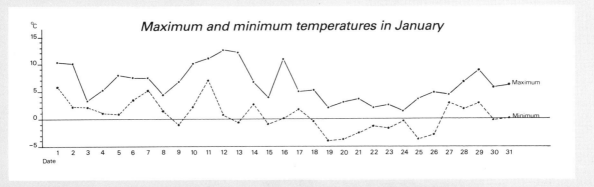

Maximum and minimum temperatures in January

B Graphs are often easier to read than a list of figures as you can quickly see changes in temperature.

1 What was the highest temperature recorded in January?

2 What was the maximum temperature recorded on 16 January?

3 How many times did the minimum temperature fall below 0°C?

4 Which was the coldest day in January?

5 On how many days did the temperature rise above 10°C? Were these warm or cold days?

6 Write one sentence to describe the weather in January.

7 What are the main differences between temperatures in January and June? Can you explain the reasons for these differences?

8 An Eskimo would probably find January's temperatures quite comfortable, yet we find them cold. Can you explain this?

Investigating Temperature

Temperatures at school

This investigation is planned to help you to record temperature conditions around your school so that you can discover how temperatures change throughout the day. Begin by drawing an outline plan of your school, like the one shown opposite. Choose about six different areas in which to record temperatures: for example, a class-room, a corridor, kitchen, library, gym and playground. Mark these areas on your map. Also mark north and the position of the morning sun. Give each area you have chosen a number and note the position of doors, windows and radiators. Place thermometers in each area and record the temperature at 9 a.m., 12 noon and 3 p.m.

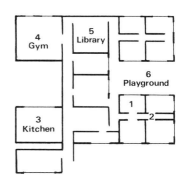

Plan of school

These results show that differences in temperature can occur in small areas. This can have a great effect on how comfortable people feel.

January

Area	9am	noon	3pm	Comment
1	10°C	20°C	18°C	Cold morning, difficult to concentrate
2	12°C	18°C	18°C	Cold all day, strong wind
3	10°C	25°C	16°C	Warmest place at lunch-time
4	9°C	21°C	17°C	P.E. soon warmed us up!
5	12°C	17°C	21°C	Warmed up after lunch
6	7°C	8°C	8°C	Cold all day, made slide during morning break

Notes: heating on, cloudy day, windows closed.

July

Area	9am	noon	3pm	Comment
1	17°C	29°C	21°C	Too hot by 10 a.m.
2	18°C	28°C	22°C	Warm and uncomfortable
3	15°C	30°C	22°C	Uncomfortable by lunch-time
4	15°C	24°C	22°C	Too warm for indoor P.E.
5	16°C	20°C	19°C	Cool and pleasant to work here
6	15°C	21°C	20°C	A warm day

Notes: heating off, all windows open, sunny day with few clouds.

Activities

A

1 Which area appears to be the warmest part of school in both January and July? Can you explain this?
2 Which area inside the school was coldest all day in January?
3 Why do you think the library was cooler than the class-rooms in July?
4 What was the coldest area of the school in: (a) January?   (b) July?
5 What could be done to improve conditions in: (a) January?   (b) July?
6 How would pupils dress for school in: (a) January?   (b) July?
7 Would these temperatures be the same on every day of January and July?

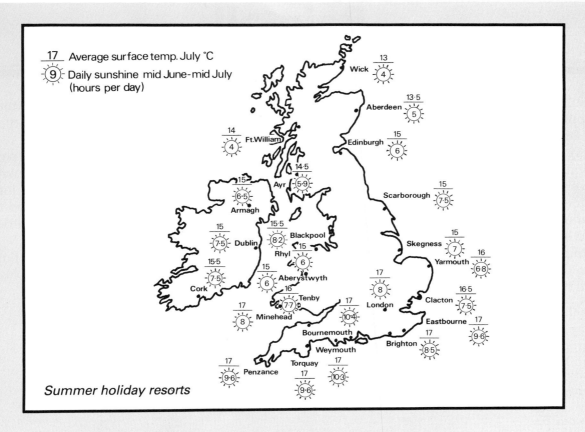

17   Average surface temp. July °C

9   Daily sunshine mid June–mid July (hours per day)

Wick 13 / 4

Aberdeen 13·5 / 5

Ft.William 14 / 4

Edinburgh 15 / 6

Ayr 14·5 / 5·9

Scarborough 15 / 7·5

Armagh 15 / 6·5

Blackpool 15·5 / 8·2

Skegness 15 / 7

Dublin 15 / 7·5

Rhyl 15 / 6

Yarmouth 16 / 6·8

Cork 15·5 / 7·5

Aberystwyth 15 / 6

London 17 / 8

Clacton 16·5 / 7·5

Tenby 16 / 7·7

Minehead 17 / 8

Bournemouth 17 / 10·4

Eastbourne 17 / 9·6

Brighton 17 / 8·5

Weymouth

Penzance 17 / 9·6

Torquay 17 / 9·6

17 / 10·3

Summer holiday resorts

B Look at the map showing average temperatures for July.

1 Which areas of Britain had the highest temperatures?

2 What do you notice about temperatures as you move north towards Scotland? Can you explain your discoveries?

Hours of sunshine are recorded on a sunshine recorder. It records only sunshine, not temperature.

3 Which place in Britain had the most sunshine in July?

4 Which place had the least sunshine in July?

5 Which coast had the most sunshine: east, south or west?

6 Write down the sunniest and cloudiest place in: (a) Scotland   (b) England   (c) Wales (d) Northern Ireland.

7 Which of the places shown would you visit for a holiday if you were given the choice? Give reasons for your answer.

8 Do you notice any similarity between hours of sunshine and temperature?

C Things to think about

1 Record the temperature and hours of sunshine for one week at your school. You will have to consider carefully how you are going to record hours of sunshine each day. Remember it is not heat you are recording but the length of time that the sun shines.

2 Use a good atlas or holiday brochures to discover July temperatures in Spain, Italy and Florida (U.S.A.). Compare these temperatures with those in Britain.

3 Newspapers sometimes give temperatures for places around the world. Collect these figures for several days. Plot the places on a world map. Record the temperatures and weather. What do you notice about: (a) nearness to the equator and temperature?   (b) temperature and general weather?

Rainfall

Rainfall has an important influence on our lives. We depend upon rainfall for our water supply. If there is too little rain people and plants may die; if there is too much rain there may be floods, which cause damage.

It is not surprising that we have so much rainfall in Britain, as we are surrounded by sea. Winds blowing across the sea pick up invisible moisture called water vapour, which slowly rises from the sea. As the water vapour rises higher it becomes cooler and condenses into tiny droplets of water which form clouds. When these clouds reach land they are forced to rise over any hills or mountains and they become cooler. The droplets of water grow larger and heavier, eventually falling to the ground as rain.

Most of the rain that falls to the ground drains into streams and rivers that eventually flow into the sea. Evaporation (water vapour rising from the sea, lakes and vegetation) takes place and the whole process begins again.

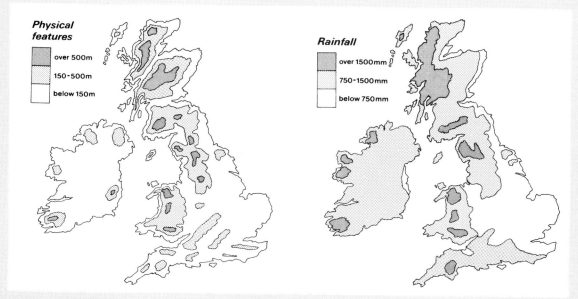

Activities

A These two maps show Britain's physical features and rainfall. They should help you to understand more about our rainfall patterns. Look carefully at the maps then answer these questions. An atlas will be needed.

1 What is similar about these two maps?

2 Which side of Britain has the most rainfall?

3 Which side of Britain has the highest mountains?

4 Why do you think western Britain has more rainfall than eastern Britain?

5 How much more rain does Fort William have than Edinburgh?

6 How much more rain does Ilfracombe have than Norwich?

7 Where does the moisture come from which gives us our rainfall? Describe carefully how it reaches the land and causes rain. You could use a diagram to show this.

Measuring rainfall

Rain is measured with a rain-gauge. This is a metal cylinder containing a funnel at the top and a container below. The base of the cylinder is sunk into the ground. When rain falls into the funnel it drains into the container. Once a day the rain-gauge is emptied into a glass measuring cylinder so that the amount of rainfall can be measured. Rainfall is measured in millimetres (mm). You can see that the measuring cylinder in the picture is marked in millimetres and centimetres.

Snow has to be melted before it can be measured. It takes 10 mm of snow to make 1 mm of water. To melt the snow, in cold countries gauges are electrically heated.

A rain-gauge has to be kept away from buildings and trees and should be surrounded by grass or gravel. Can you think why?

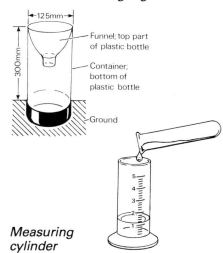

Home-made rain-gauge

Measuring cylinder

A class of children recorded the rainfall on each day during March. Here are their results.

Date	Rainfall (mm)	Date	Rainfall (mm)	Date	Rainfall (mm)	Date	Rainfall (mm)	Date	Rainfall (mm)
1	1	8	0	15	0	22	0	29	1
2	1	9	0	16	0	23	10.5	30	2
3	0.5	10	2.5	17	0	24	5	31	0
4	2	11	4.5	18	0	25	7		
5	0.5	12	0.5	19	0	26	1		
6	0	13	0.5	20	0	27	3		
7	0	14	0	21	0	28	0.5		

Rainfall is usually recorded on a block graph. Here is a block graph for the rainfall during January.

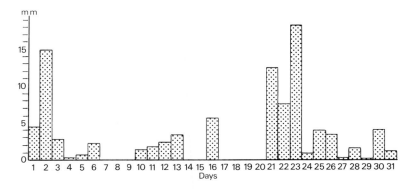

B Look carefully at the graph of January's rainfall and answer these questions.

1 On how many days was there no rainfall?

2 On how many days was there more than 5 mm of rainfall?

3 Draw a block graph of the rainfall for March.

4 Was January a wetter or drier month than March?

5 Look at the illustrations on page 5. For each one say whether or not rain would be acceptable, giving reasons for your answers.

6 Make your own rainfall records for one month and draw a block graph of your results. Compare them with the graphs for January and March.

7 We need to use the word precipitation rather than rainfall when describing January's weather. Why is this?

8 On 23 January there was snow, giving 18.4 mm of precipitation. How much snow fell?

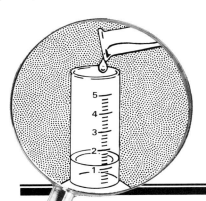

Investigating Rainfall

When it rains does the same amount of rain fall everywhere or does one area around your school receive more rainfall than another? This investigation is designed to help you discover the answer to this question. You will need some jam jars and a measuring cylinder or some plastic rain-gauges. You must then decide where to place your rain-gauges. Here are some suggestions.

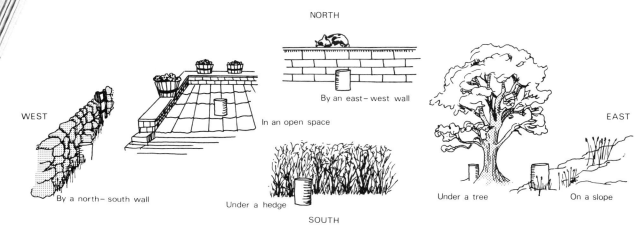

You should also record the wind direction as this may influence your results. Put the rain-gauges out at 9 a.m. and record your results at 3 p.m. You should do this every day for a week, then record your results on a chart like the one below.

Site	Total rainfall	Notes
East–west wall	7.5 mm	Main wind direction: south-west
North–south wall	2.0 mm	
Hedge	2.3 mm	Total rainfall recorded at nearest official weather station: 7.1 mm
Tree	5.5 mm	
Slope	6.8 mm	
Open space	7.0 mm	

Activities

A Using the chart above, answer these questions.
1 Can you give reasons for these results?
2 What do the results tell us about rainfall totals in a small area?
3 If the wind was blowing from a different direction would the total amounts of rainfall collected be the same if 7.1 mm was once again recorded at the local official weather station.

Holiday resorts: monthly rainfall totals, May–August

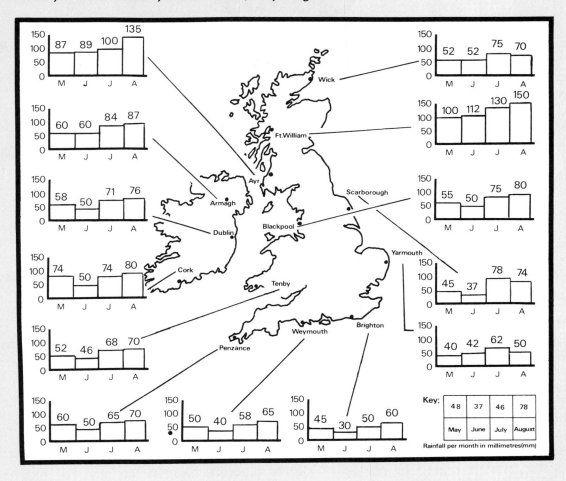

B The map above shows rainfall recorded at British holiday resorts during May, June, July and August.

1 Add up the total rainfall for each resort for the four months shown.
2 List the resorts in order of rainfall totals, starting with the highest figure.
3 Which is the best month to visit any of these resorts?
4 What do you notice about rainfall as you move along the south coast from Penzance to Brighton?
5 What do you notice about rainfall as you move from Tenby northwards to Fort William?
6 Which English resort has: (a) the least rainfall (b) the most rainfall in: (i) May (ii) June (iii) July (iv) August?
7 When is the best time to visit the west coast of Scotland if you want to avoid too much wet weather?
8 August appears to have the highest summer rainfall in most places and yet people often choose this month for their holidays. Can you explain this?

C Things to think about

Look back at the map showing holiday resorts around Britain (page 11). You now know both the rainfall and temperature for these places.

Do high temperature and low rainfall always go together? Do west coasts always have high rainfall? Can you discover any similarities between places?

Clouds

Clouds are formed when invisible particles of moisture, called water vapour, evaporate into the air from the sea, lakes, rivers and plants. As the water vapour rises it is cooled and eventually condenses back into drops of water. As these drops increase in number they bump into each other and join together, forming clouds. When the droplets become too heavy to stay in the air they fall as rain.

A boiling kettle shows clearly how clouds are formed.

Cloud formed as hot water vapour cools upon leaving kettle

Cloud types
There are several different types of clouds. They can be identified by various features: height, shape and the weather they produce.

Shape
Clouds that look like heaps of cotton wool are called **cumulus**. They have flat bases and tops shaped like cauliflowers.
Layers of cloud, which may cover the whole sky, are called **stratus**.
Clouds that look like bunches of long white threads are called **cirrus**.

Height
Layer clouds (**stratus**) are low in the sky.
The bases of heaped-up clouds (**cumulus**) are low, but they may tower to great heights.
The prefix 'alto' is added to names of clouds that are high in the sky. For example, **altocumulus** are high cumulus clouds.
White feathery **cirrus** clouds are very high up.

The weather they produce
The dark grey clouds that give rain are called **nimbus**. The word is usually combined with one of the other cloud names to describe the type of rain-cloud, e.g. **nimbostratus**, which is a layer cloud giving rain.

Cloud cover
As well as recording the type of cloud we also need to know how much of the sky is covered by cloud. We estimate this by dividing the sky into eight sections and deciding how many sections are covered by cloud. For example, if half of the sky is covered we record 4/8; if the whole sky is covered we write 8/8; 0 means a clear sky.

Here are some results taken over ten days.

Day	Cloud cover (1/8)	Day	Cloud cover (1/8)
1	8	6	7
2	7	7	8
3	4	8	0
4	5	9	8
5	3	10	2

Activities

A

1 What type of cloud do you think cumulonimbus would be?

2 What name do we give to a cloud which is high in the sky, made up of ice crystals and forms a layer across the sky?

3 Look out of the window and describe the clouds you see. Can you work out what type of clouds they are?

B Look carefully at the diagrams below. The information on the previous page should help you to name each of the cloud types numbered 1–8.

C

1 What is the name of the invisible particles of moisture which rise into the air from the sea, lakes and rivers?

2 Why do these particles become visible again?

3 How do the droplets of water in clouds grow in size?

4 Explain how a boiling kettle shows how clouds are formed.

5 What features of clouds enable us to identify them?

6 Look at the chart above.

  (a) On how many days was the sky completely covered?

  (b) On how many days was there a clear sky?

  (c) On which day was only half the sky covered?

  (d) On how many days was less than half the sky covered?

7 Draw up a chart like the one below to record cloud type and cover during one week.

Day	Cloud type and amount at			Notes
	9.00	12.00	3.00	
Monday	None	Cumulus	Stratocumulus	Clear sky, growing darker. Rain possible later.
	0	4	7	

Investigating Clouds

Clouds help us to predict what the weather is going to be like. The appearance of certain clouds usually means that a particular type of weather will follow.

Here are some ideas to test.

- Small fluffy cumulus clouds mean dry weather.
- When cirrus clouds cover the sky, a period of rain is due in the next twelve hours.
- Large, very full cumulus clouds in the afternoon mean heavy showers. There may be thunder, lightning and hail.
- Low, grey stratus clouds early in the morning mean a bright but showery afternoon.

A group of children recorded the clouds and weather for May. These were their results.

	Small fluffy cumulus clouds mean dry weather	Cirrus covering the sky means rain later	Tall cumulus in afternoon means heavy showers	Stratus in early morning means a bright showery afternoon
No. of times right	ɪɪɪ̶ I	ɪɪɪ̶ II	IIII	III
No. of times wrong		II	I	III

Activities

A

1 Which one of the ideas worked perfectly?
2 Which one of the ideas was right for only half of the time?
3 What weather seems to be linked to cirrus clouds?

B Things to think about

1 Try the same test for your own area. Do it during different months. Do you get different results in the winter?
2 Test some of the old weather sayings, e.g. 'Red sky at night, shepherd's delight.' 'Red sky in the morning, shepherd's warning.' See if you can find out any others.
3 Clouds often influence temperature. Keep a record of the cloud cover each night for a week and each morning note the minimum temperature. Compare your results.

Investigating Thunderstorms

Thunderstorms occur most often in the summer. They usually happen during the afternoon and early evening on hot days. The clouds are cumulonimbus which build up to a great height in the sky. The rainfall can be very heavy, and hailstones may fall.

Lightning is a big spark caused by static electricity in the clouds. There are two types of lightning. Sheet lightning is between one cloud and another. Forked lightning reaches the ground.

Lightning is very hot and can start fires on the ground. The heat of the flash makes the air expand suddenly, producing the noise we call thunder.

An interesting investigation is to plot the passage of a thunderstorm by recording certain features of the storm.

1 How far away the lightning is. Count the number of seconds between the flash of lightning and the thunder. The sound of thunder travels 333 metres in a second. So for every three seconds the lightning is 1 kilometre away.
2 The amount of rain every 10 minutes.
3 The strength of the wind.

Warning   Working outside when lightning is close can be dangerous.

The results of one storm are shown below.

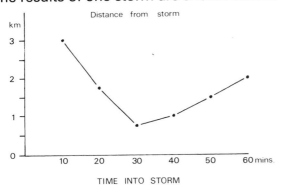

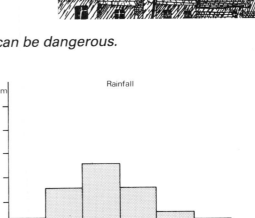

Activities

A

1 How near to the school did the thunderstorm come?
2 When did most rain fall – when the storm was closest or furthest away?
3 How much rainfall was there altogether?

B   Things to think about

1 Lightning is most likely to strike tall buildings, like church towers. How do we try to protect these buildings? (Your school may have one of these on the roof.)
2 Why do we see the lightning flash before hearing the thunder?
3 Look in a reference book to find out record amounts of rainfall, sizes of large hailstones and the power of lightning.

Wind

Wind is air moving. Air moves because the amount of it varies from one place to another. It moves from places where there is a lot of air to places where there is not so much air. Air pressure can be measured in millibars by using a barometer.

When the wind blows two things should be clear to us: how strongly it is blowing (wind speed); which direction it is blowing from (wind direction).

RECORDING WIND CONDITIONS

Speed

Wind speed is usually given as a force number which corresponds to a range of kilometres per hour. A wind scale that is commonly used has forces ranging from 0 to 12, though winds of more than 10 are very uncommon. Whatever measuring method is used it is important to agree on how strong the winds have to be for each number on the scale. Once this is established then the wind speed can be described by the force number and can be recorded easily. (See page 22.)

Measuring wind speed

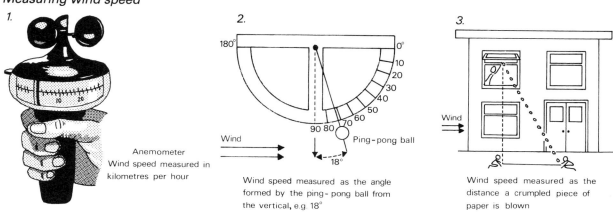

1. Anemometer
Wind speed measured in kilometres per hour

2. Wind speed measured as the angle formed by the ping-pong ball from the vertical, e.g. 18°

3. Wind speed measured as the distance a crumpled piece of paper is blown

Direction

This can be recorded by using a compass. The wind direction is the direction *from* which the wind is blowing.

Measuring wind direction

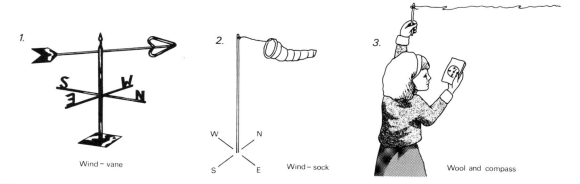

1. Wind-vane

2. Wind-sock

3. Wool and compass

A class of children made this record of the wind conditions at midday throughout the month of April. The wind force ranged from 0 (for no wind) to 5 (about 40 km/hour), the maximum speed they measured. In order to study the record more clearly they made two bar charts, one to show the frequency of wind direction and one to show the frequency of wind force.

Frequency of wind direction in April

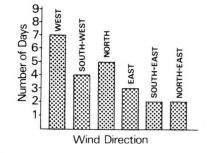

Frequency of wind force in April

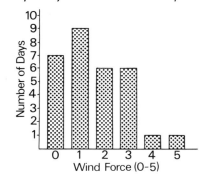

Wind record for April

Date	Direction	Force: 0 to 5	Date	Direction	Force: 0 to 5
1	West	2	16		0
2	West	3	17	South-east	2
3	South-west	1	18	South-east	2
4	South-west	1	19	East	3
5	South-west	1	20	East	3
6		0	21	North	3
7		0	22	North	2
8	North	3	23	North-east	2
9	North	3	24	North-east	1
10	East	4	25		0
11	North	5	26		0
12		0	27		0
13	West	1	28	West	1
14	South-west	2	29	West	1
15	West	1	30	West	1

Activities

Look at the wind record table for April and the two frequency bar charts.
1 Which wind direction was most common?
2 From which of the eight main compass directions did the wind not blow?
3 Which wind force was most common?
4 Which wind forces were least common?
5 From which direction did the strongest wind come?
6 Which direction always gave a force above 2?
7 Which directions always gave a force below 3?
8 Was April a windy month or was it fairly calm?
Keep your own record of the wind for a month. Use one of the methods shown on page 20 to work out a scale for measuring the strength of the wind. Once your record is complete organize the information so that it is clear to interpret. The wind rose below may be useful.

In order to combine all this information on one chart, meteorologists often draw wind-roses. These can be drawn in several ways but usually each day's wind force is written on the correct compass line for its direction. All that is lost in this form of recording are the dates when each wind occurred.

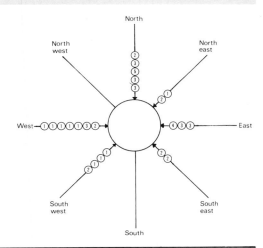

Wind-rose for the month of April

Investigating Wind

Using a wind scale to investigate wind speed

In the early nineteenth century Sir Francis Beaufort worked out a system for judging wind speed. He was an admiral in the navy and wanted a guide to wind speed that ships at sea could use. He made up a scale of 13 points (0 to 12) and at each point he gave the wind a number, a name, a range of speeds and a description of its effects. The scale was named after him.

Below is a modern version of the Beaufort scale.

Here is an example of a wind scale that a group of children invented. They did not need one as extensive as the Beaufort scale. They judged the wind speed by measuring the angle it moved a ping-pong ball from the vertical (see diagram on page 20).

Force no.	Wind name	Speed km/hr	Description of effects
0	Calm	0	Smoke rises vertically.
1	Light air	1–5	Smoke drift but no wind vane movement.
2	Light breeze	6–11	Wind felt on face. Leaves rustle. Wind vane moves.
3	Gentle breeze	12–19	Leaves and twigs in constant motion. Light flags extend.
4	Moderate breeze	20–28	Dust and loose paper raised. Small branches move.
5	Fresh breeze	29–38	Small trees begin to sway. Crested waves on inland waters.
6	Strong breeze	39–49	Large branches move. Whistling in telegraph wires. Umbrellas used with difficulty.
7	Moderate gale	50–61	Whole trees in motion. Difficult to walk against.
8	Fresh gale	62–74	Twigs break off trees. Walking very difficult.
9	Strong gale	75–88	Slight damage to buildings (chimney pots and slates removed).
10	Whole gale	89–102	Trees uprooted. Considerable damage to buildings.
11	Storm	103–117	Very rare. Widespread damage.
12	Hurricane	118+	Severe destruction.

Force no.	Wind name	Speed: angle of ping–pong ball	Description of wind effect
0	Calm	0°	No movement. Air very still everywhere.
1	Gentle breeze	0° to 10°	Tree tops move slightly. Moves a hand-held handkerchief.
2	Light wind	10° to 20°	Moves wet washing on line. Moves the weather-vane. Hair is disturbed.
3	Moderate wind	20° to 30°	Washing waves on line. Blows hair about, makes clothes flap.
4	Full wind	30° to 40°	Blows litter about. Washing blows up on line.
5	Strong wind	Over 40°	Blows litter into the air. Trees bend, large branches move in wind's direction.

Activities

A

1 Look at these pictures and put them in order to form a wind scale.

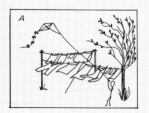

2 Describe what happens to the following as the wind gets stronger:
  (a) games (b) trees (c) washing.
3 Make your own observations of how different wind speeds can be judged. Record what happens in the area around your school and measure the speed of the winds that cause different things to happen.

How does the wind vary around buildings?

When wind speed and wind direction are measured we would expect to find fairly even results at any one time. For example, we usually expect the wind to blow with a constant speed or in gusts of constant speed, and to come from one general direction. However, buildings can make the wind behave quite differently. They can cause it to change direction, slow down or speed up.

The results below were recorded in eight different places around a school one morning. The school was well clear of other buildings and trees. The positions where the wind was measured are marked (a) to (h) on both the plan and the table.

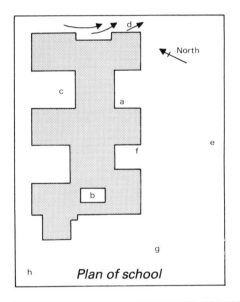

Plan of school

Position	Force no. (0–5)	Direction/description
a	2	South – east
b	0	Calm
c	4	Circling 'whirlwind'
d	3	North – west
e	3	North
f	1	East
g	2	North – east
h	3	North

B
1 Which two positions gave the same wind direction and wind speed?
2 Which two positions gave the strongest and lightest wind speeds?
3 From which general direction did the wind most often come: North, South, East or West?
4 In which positions would the building have least effect on the wind?
5 In which positions would it have most effect?
6 Why do you think the wind at (a) and (c) behaved as it did?
7 Why was the wind at (f) lighter than the wind at (g)?
8 Copy the outline of the school building and draw arrows to show how the wind pattern might be formed at each position. Position (d) has been done for you.

C Find out how the wind varies around your school. It is a good idea to check the wind speed and direction well away from the building first so that the changes the building makes are clear. When you have carried out your survey decide the best places to:
(i) have a picnic; (ii) play cards; (iii) fly a kite; (iv) read a comic; (v) play badminton; (vi) dry some washing.

Weather Forecasting

We are often interested in knowing what the weather is going to be like. Information about weather patterns is collected by various means and all this information is gathered together by one central meteorological office. From there a very detailed weather forecast is made. Newspapers, television, radio and other organizations then publish the weather forecast, but they do this in very different ways.

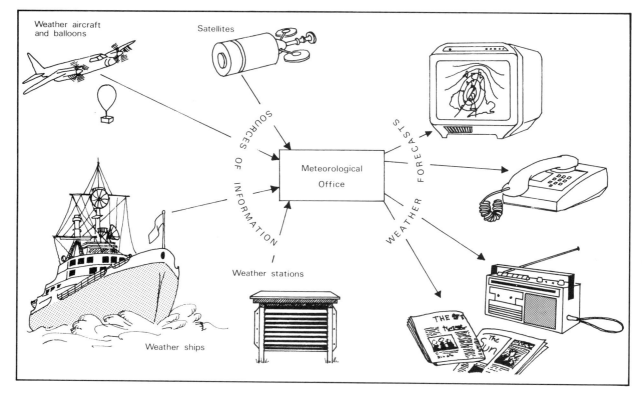

The way in which the weather forecast is presented depends on two things:
 (1) the area in which the forecast will be heard or read;
 (2) the kind of weather information listeners or readers will be most interested in knowing.

Television gives fairly detailed weather forecasts. Maps and symbols and written words can be used and there is sound so that everything can be explained. Television channels that broadcast nationally have to give an overall weather forecast, but those channels that are regional can give a more specific local forecast.

Radio Like television, radio stations use national or regional forecasts depending upon the area they are broadcasting to. Unlike television, the radio has no way of showing weather information visually, so it has to give a detailed spoken forecast.

Telephone forecasts Weather forecasting services are available over the telephone. They usually provide specific forecasting for such things as sport or road conditions.

Newspapers The amount of detail given in these forecasts varies greatly from one newspaper to another. Examples of newspaper forecasts are investigated on the next page.

Here are four weather forecasts taken from different national newspapers on the same day. It can be seen that two are extremely simple whilst the other two attempt to forecast in greater detail for different regions of the country.

The Times

Weather

A ridge of high pressure will build over Britain from N but a trough of low pressure will move N over France and into the English Channel later.

London, East Anglia, E Midlands, E, central N England: Dry, sunny periods, mist and fog patches early and late, wind variable, light; max temp 9 to 11C (48 to 52F).

SE, central S England, Channel Islands: Dry, sunny periods after early mist and fog patches, perhaps a little rain in coastal areas during the evening, wind E or NE, light or moderate, locally fresh later; max temp 10 to 12C (50 to 54F).

W Midlands, SW, NW England, Wales: Dry, sunny periods, mist and fog patches early and late; wind NE, light or moderate; max temp 9 to 11C (48 to 52F).

Lake District, Isle of Man, SW Scotland, Glasgow, Northern Ireland: Mostly dry, sunny periods, mist and fog patches early and late; wind NE to E, light; max temp 8 to 10C (46 to 50).

NE England, Borders, Edinburgh, Dundee: Isolated showers, sunny periods; wind NW, moderate, becoming variable, light; max temp 7 to 9C (45 to 48F).

Aberdeen, central Highlands, Moray Firth, NE, NW Scotland, Argyll, Orkney, Shetland: Sunny intervals, showers, snow over hills; wind NW, moderate, occasionally fresh, becoming variable, light; max temp 6 to 8C (43 to 46F).

Outlook for tomorrow and Wednesday: Mostly dry with sunny intervals in N, occasional rain in S; rather cold, with overnight frost and fog.

SEA PASSAGES: S North Sea: Wind variable, light, becoming E, moderate; sea smooth becoming slight. **Strait of Dover:** Wind SE, light, becoming E, fresh; sea smooth, becoming moderate. **English Channel (E):** Wind E, moderate of fresh, locally strong; sea moderate, locally rough. **St George's Channel, Irish Sea:** Wind light or moderate; sea slight.

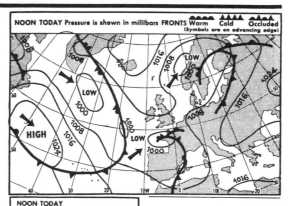

NOON TODAY Pressure is shown in millibars FRONTS Warm Cold Occluded
(Symbols are on advancing edge)

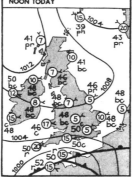

NOON TODAY

b–blue sky; bc–blue sky and cloud; c–cloudy; o–overcast; f–fog; d–drizzle; h–hail; m–mist; r–rain; s–snow; th–thunderstorm; p–showers. Arrows show wind direction, wind speed (mph) circled. temperatures fahrenheit.

Daily Express

Sunny spells after fog.
Outlook: Dry, sunny.

● 1, 3, 5, 6, 7, 9, 10, 11, 12, 15 : Dry, sunny periods. Mist and fog early and late. Max 11C (52F).

● 2, 4, 8 : Dry, sunny periods after early mist. Perhaps a little rain on coast later. Max 12C (54F).

● 13, 14, 20, 21, 29 : Mostly dry, sunny periods. Mist and fog early and late. Max 10C (50F).

● 16, 17, 18 : Isolated showers. Sunny periods. Max 9C (49F).

● 19, 22, 23, 24, 25, 26, 27, 28 : Sunny intervals, showers, with snow over hills. Max 8C (46F).

Sun sets 4.27 p.m., rises 7.02 a.m. tomorrow. Moon rises 3.41 p.m., sets 4.16 a.m. tomorrow. London lighting-up time : 4.56 p.m. to 6.33 a.m. tomorrow. High water at London Bridge : 11.49 a.m. and 12.19 a.m. tomorrow.

Activities

A

1 Which newspaper tells you most about the weather?
2 Which is easiest to read?
3 What weather did each newspaper forecast for London?
4 What was the forecast for your area?
5 If you lived in northern Scotland which newspapers would you find most useful and least useful?
6 Do they all give the same general forecast?
7 Which newspaper do you think gives the most useful forecast? What are your reasons?

B   Things to think about

1 Listen to this evening's radio or television forecast and write a forecast suitable for publication in: (a) *The Times* (b) the *Sun*.
2 Why do many people prefer weather forecasts like those in the *Sun*?
3 Which people are most likely to need detailed weather forecasts? (Example: farmers.) Give your reasons.

Daily Mirror

Weather

TODAY: Cloudy with rain. Cold. Max temp 9C (48F). TOMORROW: Similar.

Sun

WEATHER

DRY and sunny in most areas. Northern England and Scotland will have wintry showers.
OUTLOOK: Similar, but getting colder.
SUN rises 7.01am, sets 4.26pm. **LIGHTS:** 4.56pm to 6.31am.

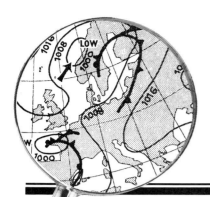

Investigating
Weather Forecasting

How accurate do the forecasts need to be?

The detailed weather forecasts given on Radio 4 are said to be correct nine times out of ten. To find out the accuracy of different forecasts a school carried out a survey over five days. Forecasts from the following sources were used: a popular newspaper (the *Sun*); a serious newspaper (*The Times*); Radio 4; local radio; ITV.

At the end of the day the actual weather conditions recorded at the school were entered in the table. Where the forecasts gave regional variations then the local one was used for this investigation.

	Temperature (maximum)					Conditions					Wind				
Sun	22	22	20	18	17	Sunny and dry	Sunny spells	Wet	Wet	Wet	W	W	NW	—	—
The Times	20	20	19	17	16	Cloudy, outbreaks of rain	Cloudy with heavy showers	High pressure declining	Low trough – rain	Drizzle	W	W	W	S	—
Radio 4	21	21	20	17	16	Bright with showers	Sunny periods with showers	Mainly wet with some sun	Overcast with intermittent rain	Rain, cloudy	W	W	—	—	—
Local radio	20	19	19	18	15	Sunny periods, showers	Light rain with heavier outbursts	Some rain with bright periods	Isolated showers	Showers and sunny spells	W	W	NW	—	—
ITV	19	17	18	17	16	Sunny periods and light showers	Rain from the West	Blue skies with increasing cloud	Heavy rain in places	Rain with some sun	W	W	NW	—	—
School record	21	20	18	17	16	Sunny and dry	Sunny morning, rain later	Wet all day	Steady rain	Heavy showers	W	W	W	No wind	No wind

Activities

A

1 Are all the forecasts similar?

2 Which forecasts were most accurate and which was least accurate for temperature?

3 Which was the most useful in forecasting weather conditions? Why?

4 Score each forecast against the school record so that its accuracy can be measured.

5 Which forecast do you think was most accurate and which one least accurate for this area?

B Now do a survey of your own to find out the accuracy of different forecasts. It will be necessary to work out the main points from the forecasts and not be confused by the many 'ifs' and 'buts' that are often included. If possible, you could record the radio and television forecasts to help you remember the details.

Some weather forecasts may be for a much wider area than your own region so you should expect your weather record to be different from the broad forecasts.

Investigating Weather Lore

Before radio and television were invented and newspapers were published, there were no weather forecasts available. However, people learnt, by studying the natural world around them, that certain things happened when the weather was about to change. These signs became part of our weather lore.

Below is a list of signs that are used for forecasting rain. Perhaps you already know some of them or even know of other signs of your own.

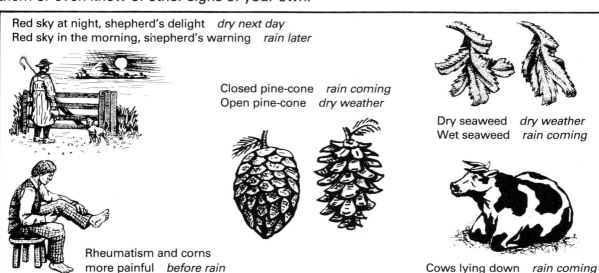

Red sky at night, shepherd's delight   *dry next day*
Red sky in the morning, shepherd's warning   *rain later*

Closed pine-cone   *rain coming*
Open pine-cone   *dry weather*

Dry seaweed   *dry weather*
Wet seaweed   *rain coming*

Rheumatism and corns more painful   *before rain*

Cows lying down   *rain coming*

C Which signs are most reliable? Make a table like the one below and collect the objects you need so that you can keep a check on them to tell whether or not it may rain. Include any other ideas you know. You will also need to keep a record of the weather. Keep a tally of how many times each sign seemed to work and how many times it did not, like this:

	Sign indicates	Actual weather	No. of times it worked	No. of times it didn't work
Red sky				
Pine-cone				
Seaweed				
Corns/rheumatism				
Cows				
Halo round the moon				

- From your observations which signs do you think you can rely on most?
- Which is the least reliable?
- Which method of forecasting is most fun: using old signs or following modern scientific measuring methods?

Useful Data Collection and Classification Sheets

A daily record sheet is useful for collecting all the measurable information in one place.

Day		Temperature Max.°C Min.°C		Wind Direction Speed		Rainfall mm	Cloud Cover Type		Humidity
	a.m.								
	p.m.								
	a.m.								
	p.m.								
	a.m.								
	p.m.								
	a.m.								
	p.m.								

Relative humidity

To measure the relative humidity of the air we compare the temperature recorded on a dry bulb thermometer with that recorded on a wet bulb thermometer.

Example   The dry bulb thermometer reads   22°C
The wet bulb thermometer reads   18°C
The difference in temperature is   4°C

By using the relative humidity table as shown, it can be seen that the relative humidity of the air is 68%.

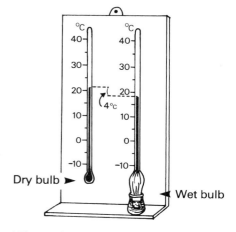

Dry bulb ►

◄ Wet bulb

How to use a relative humidity table

Wet and dry bulb thermometer

Difference is 4°C ▼

Dry bulb reading	0.5	1.0	1.5	2.0	2.5	3.0	3.5	4.0	4.5	5.0	5.5	6.0	6.5	7.0	7.5	8.0	8.5	9.0
	%	%	%	%	%	%	%	%	%	%	%	%	%	%	%	%	%	%
24	96	92	88	84	80	77	73	69	66	62	59	56	52	49	46	43	40	37
22	96	92	87	83	79	76	72	68	64	61	57	54	50	47	44	40	37	34
20	96	91	86	83	78	74	70	66	62	59	55	51	48	44	41	37	34	30
18	95	91	86	82	77	73	69	65	60	56	55	48	45	41	37	34	30	27
16	95	90	85	81	76	71	67	62	58	54	50	46	41	37	34	30	26	22
14	95	90	84	79	74	70	65	60	56	51	47	42	38	33	29	25	24	17
12	94	89	83	78	73	68	60	57	53	48	43	38	34	29	24	20	16	11
10	94	88	82	76	71	65	59	54	49	44	39	34	29	24	19	14	9	5
8	94	87	81	75	69	63	57	51	46	40	35	29	23					
6	93	86	79	73	66	60	53	47	41	35	29	23						
4	92	85	78	70	63	56	49	42	36	29	22							
2	92	84	76	68	60	52	45	37	30	22								
0	91	82	73	65	56	48	39	31	22									

Dry bulb ► reading is 22°C

Relative humidity of the air is 68%

A visual way of recording weather conditions is simply by using symbols instead of numerical information. While it is important that children learn to recognize the correct weather symbols, they should also be encouraged to make up their own (e.g. sunny day and cloud on symbols diagram). This could lead to a discussion about conventional symbols.

Symbols for use on daily record chart

●	Rain
▽	Showers
✿	Snow
⊼	Thunderstorm
═	Fog
⑮	Temperature
☀	Sunny day
N.E.	Wind direction
☁	Cloud size = cover
⌄	Wind

Up to four of these symbols could be used to record visually each day's weather, as shown below.

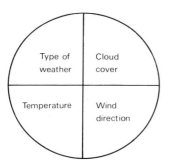

Daily record chart

Monday	Tuesday	Wednesday	Thursday	Friday
● ☁ ⑮ S.W.	▽ ☁ ⑯ S.W.	☀ ㉕ S.		

Commercially produced weather boards can be a useful method of presenting data.

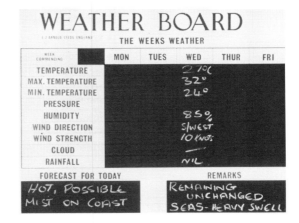

Various styles of weather map appear on television and in weather reports. The map below is the type used in the Meteorological Office.

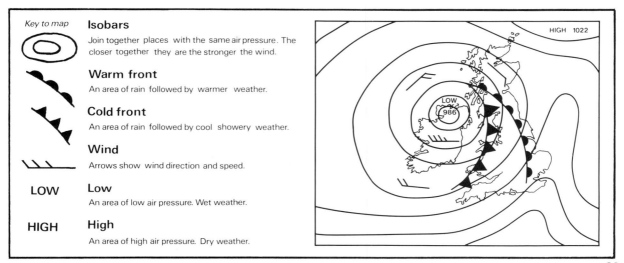

Notes for Teachers

AIMS   This book aims to:

- provide stimulus material which will lead children into studying the weather in their environment.
- develop the concepts and skills listed below through direct observation, practical investigation, measurement and information sorting.
- provide key information that is essential in studying elements of the weather.
- develop powers of deduction so that patterns and trends can be seen in the weather and further interpretations made.
- provide a background vocabulary and knowledge from which to work.

SKILLS   This book helps children to develop skills in:

- measuring weather conditions using conventional instruments and simple devices.
- conducting field investigations in order to gather information.
- recording measurements in appropriate tabulated and pictorial forms so that interpretation can be properly attempted.
- recognizing, understanding and using standard symbols to record aspects of the weather.
- interpreting recorded weather data so that patterns and sequences can be recognized.
- identifying the factors that cause certain weather conditions.

CONCEPTS   The book leads children towards developing concepts about:

- the elements that make up the weather.
- the effects of weather on our daily lives.
- how weather conditions can be measured in very different but equally valid ways.
- the interrelation of different aspects of the weather.
- how weather patterns and sequences enable forecasts to be made.
- how local weather may vary from wider patterns.

ATTITUDES AND VALUES   The work in this book should foster:

- an attitude of curiosity which helps enquiry into the weather of the immediate environment.
- an inventiveness towards ways of measuring weather conditions.
- a desire to probe for reasons and explanations of why certain weather conditions exist and how these affect us.
- an active and critical approach to data interpretation.
- a disciplined and conscientious approach to research work.

Implementation

USING THIS BOOK Each section provides sufficient material to allow work to be undertaken solely from the book. Using the ideas and information in these pages teachers can lead children into investigations and interpretations immediately in the class-room. However, the intention is that children should venture out and pursue the kind of weather research that the different sections suggest. Background vocabulary and basic knowledge is given so that children can move into the essence of their work directly and without the distractions and frustrations that field-work can so often incur.

MIXED ABILITY The work is designed to cater for children of all abilities working in the same class. The information given is of easy readability and the tasks and recording techniques suggested are clear and straightforward. The development of the investigations allows active participation by the least able, whilst the most able children are led into more challenging situations. Theories and hypotheses are usually neither right nor wrong, rather there are solutions which are more or less acceptable depending upon the quality, accuracy and reliability of the evidence and the judgement upon which they are based. The better the evidence then the stronger the work will be. It is of great educational value if children can themselves observe, measure and test to find evidence that can be used to support or challenge their view. Weaknesses, shortcomings and inconsistencies in the evidence should also be pointed out.

At all ability levels children should be encouraged throughout this work to seek out patterns of similarity and difference, continuity and change and cause and effect.

PAGE BY PAGE

6 and 7 Other styles of weather map exist (as shown on page 29). The maps on this page are simple and straightforward and may be easier to interpret than many that can be found.

8 and 9 Temperature is concerned with degrees of hotness and coldness and degrees Celsius should be used exclusively.

10 and 11 The point to be made is that temperature varies over small areas, regions and on a world scale.

12 and 13 Relief maps and rainfall maps show similar patterns. Children need some idea of how much rainfall corresponds, for example, to 5 mm.

14 and 15 Wind direction will need to be measured so it might be helpful to use pages 19–20 in conjunction with this section.

16 and 17 Answers to cloud types are: 1 Cumulonimbus, 2 Nimbostratus, 3 Cumulus, 4 Cirrus, 5 Altocumulus, 6 Altostratus, 7 Cirrostratus, 8 Stratocumulus.

20 and 21 Home-made methods of measuring are often the best ways; let children use their 'scientific imaginations'.

22 and 23 To measure variations in wind direction and speed it is important to choose a site where differences are likely to occur. General wind measurements should be taken at a distance from buildings.

26 and 27 Summarizing weather forecasts can be extremely difficult: children will need guidance.

ORGANIZATION OF TIME Good field-work takes time and so does good follow-up work. Whilst the work needs to have pace and development it does require blocks of time that extend beyond the conventional 'lesson period'. *Investigating Weather* is best used over the period of a school year so that scientific comparisons can be made. Given this, the children should develop a critical awareness and understanding beyond the ambitions of many topic-book approaches, provided that the practical aspects are applied within their own environment.

An excellent selection of weather equipment can be found in the science section of the E.J. Arnold equipment catalogue.

CROSS-CURRICULAR

Investigating Weather can be used for a variety of subjects. Weather is commonly studied in Geography and Environmental Studies, but can also provide a real-life focus for much work in Maths, Technology, and English. In addition, *Investigating Weather* helps develop scientific understanding and many skills which are appropriate for Science.

Because of the points already made, a study/topic/theme or enquiry on 'Weather' provides an ideal springboard for cross-curricular work. In addition, *Investigating Weather* appeals equally to girls and boys, from many different cultural and ethnic backgrounds.

LINKS WITH SCIENCE

Attainment Target 9: Earth and Atmosphere

The *Science document, NCC Consultation Report (December 1988)* states that pupils need to study the weather at different ages. The table below shows how pages in *Investigating Weather* can be related to the appropriate levels of attainment for Target 9:

Level	4/5	6/7	8/9	10/11	12/13	14/15	16/17	18/19	20/21	22/23	24/25	26/27	28/29
						Page numbers							
1		✓		✓		✓		✓		✓			
2	✓			✓		✓		✓		✓			
3		✓		✓		✓			✓	✓	✓	✓	✓
4				✓		✓		✓	✓	✓			
5							✓						

Attainment Target 1: Exploration of Science

In *Investigating Weather* pupils develop investigative skills and understanding of Science.

Attainment Target 2: Variety of Life

In *Investigating Weather* pupils can study a variety of localities at first hand, and through secondary sources, investigate the range of seasonal and daily variability in physical factors. They also relate environmental factors to human well-being.

Attainment Target 3: Processes of Life

In *Investigating Weather* pupils can investigate the effects of physical factors (light, temperature, etc.) on rates of plant growth.

Attainment Target 13: Energy

In *Investigating Weather* pupils are encouraged to begin to link feelings of hot and cold with temperature, measured by thermometer.

LINKS WITH MATHS

The observation and recording of data involved in weather recording leads to the drawing, and subsequent interpretation, of that data. Graphs, charts, and statistics are produced, recorded, interpreted, and used. This is often done in the context of 'real' enquiry.

LINKS WITH ENGLISH

There are a variety of opportunities for developing all four modes of language – reading, writing, speaking, and listening – in specific contexts. The activities suggested in *Investigating Weather* include describing accurately, formulating questions, organizing and sequencing information, evaluating and reflecting, and involving others in a discussion.

NB Teachers will need to check this information with the Targets and Levels in the final NCC document.